Sixth Grade Social Science Quizzes

By Terri Raymond

I0429853

Home School Brew Press
www.HomeSchoolBrew.com

© 2014. All Rights Reserved.

Cover Image © puckillustrations - Fotolia.com

Table of Contents

Disclaimer

This book was developed for parents and students of no particular state; while it is based on common core standards, it is always best to check with your state board to see what will be included on testing.

About Us

Homeschool Brew was started for one simple reason: to make affordable Homeschooling books! When we began looking into homeschooling our own children, we were astonished at the cost of curriculum. Nobody ever said homeschool was easy, but we didn't know that the cost to get materials would leave us broke.

We began partnering with educators and parents to start producing the same kind of quality content that you expect in expensive books...but at a price anyone can afford.

We are still in our infancy stages, but we will be adding more books every month. We value your feedback, so if you have any comments about what you like or how we can do better, then please let us know!

To add your name to our mailing list, go here: http://www.homeschoolbrew.com/mailing-list.html

Paleolithic-Agricultural Revolution: Quiz

(1) What primate do anthropologists believe humans evolved from?
(A) Bonobo
(B) Chimpanzee
(C) Gorilla
(D) Orangutan

(2) Early humans liked to roam from place to place, which means that they were _____.
(A) Nomadic
(B) Self-serving
(C) Farming creatures
(D) Chimpanzees

(3) On what continent did humans originate?
(A) North America
(B) Africa
(C) Asia
(D) Europe

(4) What do you call someone who studies humans, past and present?
(A) Biologist

(B) Chimpologist
(C) Homologist
(D) Anthropologist

(5) What was the first type of hominid?
(A) *Homo sapien*
(B) *Homo erectus*
(C) *Homo habilis*
(D) *Australopithecus*

(6) What type of hominid was referred to as the "handy man?"
(A) *Homo sapien*
(B) *Homo erectus*
(C) *Homo habilis*
(D) *Australopithecus*

(7) The Stone Age is a nickname for what era?
(A) The Jurassic Era
(B) The Paleomythic Era
(C) The Age of Heroes
(D) The Paleolithic Era

(8) Which hominid's name means "person who walks upright?"
(A) Neanderthal
(B) *Homo sapien*
(C) *Homo erectus*
(D) *Homo Australopithecus*

(9) Which hominid's name means "person who can think?"
(A) *Homo sapien*
(B) *Homo habilis*
(C) *Homo erectus*
(D) *Homo Neanderthalis*

(10)   What hominid do you classify as?
(A) *Homo sapien*
(B) *Homo habilis*
(C) *Homo erectus*
(D) *Homo Australopithecus*

(11)   During the Agricultural Revolution, what did hominids begin to do?
(A) Foray and hunt
(B) Bury their dead
(C) Settle and farm
(D) Heal their wounded

(12)   Anthropologists believe what hominid first started to introduce burial rites into their culture?
(A) Cro-Magnon
(B) Neanderthal
(C) *Australopithecus*
(D) *Homo sapien*

(13) Anthropologists believe what hominid was the first to settle down and start farming?
(A) Cro-Magnon
(B) Neanderthal
(C) *Australopithecus*
(D) *Homo sapien*

(14) How did humans get to North America?
(A) They sailed by boat from Europe.
(B) They sailed by boat from Africa.
(C) They crossed by land from Asia.
(D) They crossed by land from Australia.

(15) Anthropologists believe what hominid developed ways to heal itself?
(A) Cro-Magnon
(B) *Homo habilis*
(C) Neanderthal
(D) *Homo erectus*

(16) The Ice Age's massive glaciers reached every continent on the globe.
(A) True
(B) False

(17) Both plants and animals were a major part of the Agricultural Revolution for humans.
(A) True

(B) False

(18)   The Out of Africa theory has been proved undeniably true.
(A) True
(B) False

(19)   The Paleolithic Era is often called the Iron Age.
(A) True
(B) False

(20)   Early humans often wasted no part of any animal they killed.
(A) True
(B) False

Paleolithic-Agricultural Revolution: Quiz Answers

(1) **B.** Anthropologists believe humans evolved from chimpanzees.
(2) **A.** Early humans liked to roam from place to place, which means they were nomadic.
(3) **B.** Humans originated on Africa.
(4) **D.** An anthropologist studies humans, past and present.
(5) **D.** The first type of hominid was *Australopithecus*.
(6) **C.** *Homo habilis* was referred to as the "handy man."
(7) **D.** The Stone Age is a nickname for the Paleolithic Era.
(8) **C.** "Person who walks upright" is the meaning of *Homo erectus*.
(9) **A.** *Homo sapien* means "person who can think."
(10) **A.** You classify as a *homo sapien*.

(11)   **C.** During the Agricultural Revolution, humans began to settle and farm.

(12)   **B.** Anthropologists believe that Neanderthals were the first to introduce burial rites into their culture.

(13)   **A.** Anthropologists believe that the Cro-Magnons were the first to settle down and farm.

(14)   **C.** Humans reached Asia by crossing by land from Asia.

(15)   **C.** Anthropologists believe that Neanderthals developed healing methods.

(16)   **False.** The Ice Age's glaciers did not reach ever continent.

(17)   **True.** Both plants and animals were a major part of the Agricultural Revolution.

(18)   **False.** The Out of Africa theory has not been proved undeniably true; it is a theory, but a likely one.

(19)   **False.** The Paleolithic Era is often called the Stone Age, not the Iron Age.

(20)   **True.** Early humans often wasted no part of any animal they killed.

Mesopotamia, Egypt, and Kush:
Quiz

(1) Mesopotamia is often called the
   "_____ of Civilization."
   (A) Cradle
   (B) Birthplace
   (C) Origin
   (D) Catalyst

(2) What does "Mesopotamia" mean?
   (A) The Birthplace of Civilization
   (B) The Place of Royal Gods
   (C) The Land Between the Rivers
   (D) The City Beneath the Mountains

(3) How many kings did Mesopotamia have?
   (A) One
   (B) Two
   (C) Three
   (D) Four

(4) The Library of Ninevah was located in what
   area of Mesopotamia?
   (A) Babylon
   (B) Sumer
   (C) Assyria
   (D) Mesop

(5) Who was Gilgamesh?
   (A) One of Mesopotamia's famous kings, who
       led the people to success in war
   (B) One of Assyria's legendary scholars, who
       worked in the library of Ninevah
   (C) A character in an Ancient Mesopotamian
       story
   (D) A famous gladiator who fought in
       Mesopotamia's coliseum

(6) What was Hammurabi's Code?
   (A) A set of laws set down by King
       Hammurabi
   (B) The code that allowed people access into
       Hammurabi's Pyramid
   (C) The password that gave people permission
       to enter the Golden Gates of Egypt
   (D) A set of numbers and laws that gave
       Mesoptamia its library coding system

(7) Put the Mesopotamian class system in order, from *Highest Class* to *Lowest Class*.
(A) Upper Class, Lower Class, Priests, Slaves
(B) Slaves, Lower Class, Priests, Upper Class
(C) Upper Class, Priests, Lower Class, Slaves
(D) Priests, Upper Class, Lower Class, Slaves

(8) What river runs through Egypt?
(A) Tigris
(B) Euphrates
(C) Amazon
(D) Nile

(9) What were the three kingdoms of Egypt called?
(A) The Stone Kingdom, the Iron Kingdom, the Golden Kingdom
(B) The First Kingdom, the Second Kingdom, the Third Kingdom
(C) The Old Kingdom, the Middle Kingdom, the New Kingdom
(D) The Left Kingdom, the Center Kingdom, the Right Kingdom

(10)   Egypt was ruled by:
(A) A pharaoh
(B) A king
(C) A group of nobles
(D) The rich vizier

(11)   Which society gave the world advanced justice systems?
(A) Mesopotamia
(B) Kush

(C) Egypt
(D) Assyria

(12)   Which society sat between the Tigris and Euphrates Rivers?
(A) Mesopotamia
(B) Kush
(C) Egypt
(D) Babylon

(13)   What is the longest river in the world?
(A) Tigris
(B) Euphrates
(C) Amazon
(D) Nile

(14)   Kush was known as the "Land of the _____," because of _____.
(A) Ivory, because of their abundant elephants.
(B) Bow, because of their skilled archers.
(C) Sword, because of their skilled knights.
(D) Water, because of the Nile River.

(15)   Kush was ruled by a:
(A) Queen
(B) Pharaoh
(C) King
(D) Group of nobles

(16)   These civilizations took place during the Stone Age.
(A) True
(B) False

(17)   Kush worshipped a singular God.
    (A) True
    (B) False

(18)   A group of Mesopotamians traveled
    across the Sahara Desert and discovered other
    civilizations.
    (A) True
    (B) False

(19)   The Egyptians gave us papyrus, and
    early form of paper.
    (A) True
    (B) False

(20)   *Gilgamesh* is the first story recorded
    by humans.
    (A) True
    (B) False

Mesopotamia, Egypt, and Kush: Quiz Answers

(1) **A.** Mesopotamia is often called the Cradle of Civilization.

(2) **C.** Mesopotamia means "The Land Between the Rivers."

(3) **A.** Mesopotamia had one king.

(4) **C.** The Library of Ninevah was located in Assyria.

(5) **C.** Gilgamesh was a character in an Ancient Mesopotamian story.

(6) **A.** Hammurabi's Code was a set of laws set down by King Hammurabi.

(7) **D.** The class system, from highest to lowest, in Mesopotamia is: Priests, Upper Class, Lower Class, Slaves.

(8) **D.** The Nile River runs through Egypt.

(9) **C.** The three kingdoms of Egypt were the Old Kingdom, the Middle Kingdom, and the New Kingdom.

(10) **A.** Egypt was ruled by a pharaoh.

(11) **C.** Egypt gave the world advanced justice systems.

(12) **A.** Mesopotamia sat between the Tigris and Euphrates.

(13) **D.** The Nile is the longest river in the world.

(14) **B.** Kush was known as the Land of the Bow, because of the skilled archers.

(15)   **A.** Kush was ruled by a queen.

(16)   **False.** These civilizations took place during the Iron Age.

(17)   **False.** Kush worshipped multiple gods, many of them Egyptian.

(18)   **False.** Men from Kush traveled across the Sahara, not Mesopotamians.

(19)   **True.** The Egyptians gave us papyrus.

(20)   **True.** *Gilgamesh* is the first story recorded by humans.

Ancient Hebrews: Quiz

(1) What form of religion worships more than one god?
(A) Monotheistic
(B) Polytheistic
(C) Christianity
(D) Islam

(2) What form of religion worships only one god?
(A) Monotheistic
(B) Polytheistic
(C) Pentistic
(D) Mesopotamian

(3) To what country do Christianity, Judaism, and Islam have historical ties?
(A) Turkey
(B) Israel
(C) Russia
(D) Egypt

(4) Why did the Israelites leave Canaan?
(A) They were attacked by Egyptian slavers
(B) God brought many plagues down upon them
(C) They suffered a terrible drought
(D) God commanded them to leave

(5) What country took in the Israelite refugees, and then enslaved them later?
(A) Egypt

(B) Mesopotamia
(C) Kush
(D) Canaan

(6) Which of the following was NOT one of the plagues that, according to the Bible, God brought down upon the Egyptians?
(A) Locusts
(B) River of blood
(C) Eclipse of the sun and moon
(D) Termites

(7) What was the "Exodus?"
(A) The Israelite journey from Canaan to Egypt, to escape the drought
(B) The Israelite journey out of Egypt, led by Moses
(C) The Egyptian journey to Canaan, to enslave the Israelites
(D) The Israelite journey from Egypt to Kush, to find a new homeland

(8) What is the religious book of Judaism?
(A) The Bible
(B) The Quran
(C) The Torah
(D) The Book of Good and Evil

(9) What famous empire stretched across Europe, into northern Africa, and reached the eastern Mediterranean?
(A) Mesopotamian
(B) Greek
(C) Roman

(D) Egyptian

(10)   What was the Diaspora?
(A) The Israelite journey from Canaan to
    Egypt
(B) The destruction of the Library of Ninevah
(C) The destruction of Jerusalem
(D) The destruction of the Roman capital by
    the Israelites

(11)   In 1947, a set of scrolls were found
that are called the _____ Scrolls.
(A) Red Sea
(B) Dead Sea
(C) Mediterranean Sea
(D) Narrow Sea

(12)   The Dead Sea is called such, because
_____.
(A) Bodies often turn up on shore, some of
    them decades old.
(B) The salt level allows people to float, often
    making them appear "dead."
(C) The salt level is so high that no fish or
    aquatic creature can survive there.
(D) It was the sea upon which King David of
    Israel was pronounced dead.

(13)   What holiday celebrates the Jewish
New Year?
(A) *Rosh Hashanah*
(B) Torah Day
(C) The Day of Judgment
(D) *Yom Kippur*

(14)　　　What Jewish holiday is the "Day of Atonement?"
(A) *Rosh Hashanah*
(B) The Day of the Book of Good and Evil
(C) The Day of Judgment
(D) *Yom Kippur*

(15)　　　Israel sits in what part of the world?
(A) Europe
(B) Middle East
(C) Greater Asia
(D) Minor Eurasia

(16)　　　According to the Bible, King David of Israel previously killed a monster named Goliath.
(A) True
(B) False

(17)　　　Egyptians believed in a religious system of monotheism.
(A) True
(B) False

(18)　　　Today, Jews believe that Jesus Christ was the messiah.
(A) True
(B) False

(19)　　　Emperor Constantine of Rome declared that Christianity would be Rome's official religion.
(A) True

(B) False

(20)	The Ten Commandments were received by King Solomon at the peak of Mount Olympus.
(A) True
(B) False

Ancient Hebrews: Quiz Answers

(1) **B.** Polytheism means the worship of more than one god.

(2) **A.** Monotheism means the worship of only one god.

(3) **B.** Christianity, Judaism, and Islam have historical ties to Israel.

(4) **C.** The Israelites left Canaan because they suffered a terrible drought.

(5) **A.** The Egyptians took in Israelite refugees and enslaved them later.

(6) **D.** Termites was NOT one of the plagues that, according to the Bible, God brought down upon the Egyptians.

(7) **B.** The "Exodus" was the Israelite journey out of Egypt, led by Moses.

(8) **C.** The religious book of Judaism is the Torah.

(9) **C.** The Roman Empire stretched across Europe, into northern Africa, and reached the eastern Mediterranean.

(10) **C.** The Diaspora was the destruction of Jerusalem.

(11) **B.** In 1947, the Dead Sea Scrolls were found.

(12) **B.** The Dead Sea was named after the fact that the salt levels allow people to float, often making them appear "dead."

(13) **A.** *Rosh Hashanah* celebrates the Jewish New Year.

(14)   **D.** *Yom Kippur* celebrates the Day of Atonement.

(15)   **B.** Israel sits in the Middle Easts.

(16)   **True.** According to the Bible, King David of Israel previously killed a monster named Goliath.

(17)   **False.** Egyptians believed in a polytheistic system, not monotheistic.

(18)   **False.** Today, Jews do not believe that Jesus was the messiah.

(19)   **True.** Emperor Constantine declared that Rome's official religion would be Christianity.

(20)   **False.** The Ten Commandments were received by Moses on Mt. Sinai, not King Solomon on Olympus.

Ancient Greece: Quiz

(1) Ancient Greece rested on what major European sea?
(A) Baltic
(B) Black
(C) Ural
(D) Mediterranean

(2) The first period of Ancient Greece was the
_____.
(A) Classical Period
(B) Hellenistic Period
(C) Archaic Period
(D) Alexandrian Period

(3) *The Odyssey* and *The Iliad* were about what war?
(A) The Spartan Wars
(B) The Peloponnesian War
(C) The Trojan War
(D) The War of Greek Conquest

(4) The second period of Ancient Greece was the
_____.
(A) Classical Period
(B) Hellenistic Period
(C) Archaic Period
(D) Middle Period

(5) Choose the option with the Greek
philosophers in which they first appeared.
Who taught who?
(A) Plato→Socrates→Aristotle
(B) Socrates→Plato→Aristotle
(C) Aristotle→Plato→Socrates
(D) Aristotle→Socrates→Plato

(6) What war was fought between Athens and
Sparta because Athens tried to conquer other
city-states?
(A) The Trojan War
(B) The War of Spartan Defense
(C) The War of the Five Kings
(D) The Peloponnesian War

(7) Whose death ended the Classical Period?
(A) Alexander the Great
(B) Homer
(C) Jesus Christ
(D) Socrates

(8) The third and final period of Ancient Greece
was called the _____.
(A) Archaic Period
(B) Classical Period
(C) Hellenistic Period
(D) New Period

(9) How many *Olympians* were there in Greek
mythology?
(A) Over one hundred
(B) Twelve
(C) Ten

(D) Fifteen

(10)   Who wrote *The Odyssey* and *The Iliad*?
(A) Socrates
(B) Homer
(C) Plato
(D) Alexander the Great

(11)   What impact did the Greeks have on our modern court system?
(A) Trial by jury
(B) A judge to preside over the trial
(C) Allowing citizens to watch the trial
(D) Limiting jail sentences to thirty-five years for minor crimes

(12)   What did the Greeks call themselves?
(A) Greeks
(B) Grecians
(C) Hellens
(D) Hellenistics

(13)   Who was the ruler of the Greek gods?
(A) Hades
(B) Zeus
(C) Hero
(D) Ares

(14)   What is an *acropolis*?
(A) A temple to worship the gods
(B) An elevated area of land
(C) A city hall in Ancient Greece

(D) A mountain where the Grecians believed
the gods lived

(15)   What form of religion did the Ancient
Grecians follow?
(A) Monotheistic
(B) Polytheistic
(C) They had no form of religion
(D) Everyone followed a different belief
system

(16)   Alexander the Great was from
Macedonia.
(A) True
(B) False

(17)   The Ancient Grecians used gods and
goddesses to explain the way the world
worked around them.
(A) True
(B) False

(18)   Athens won the Peloponnesian War.
(A) True
(B) False

(19)   Alexander the Great failed to spread
Greek culture during his conquests throughout
Eurasia.
(A) True
(B) False

(20)   The Ancient Greeks conquered the
Roman Empire.

(A) True
(B) False

Ancient Greece: Quiz Answers

(1) **D.** Ancient Greece rested on the Mediterranean Sea.

(2) **C.** The first period of Ancient Greece was the Archaic Period.

(3) **C.** *The Odyssey* and *The Iliad* were about the Trojan War.

(4) **A.** The second period of Ancient Greece was the Classical Period.

(5) **B.** Socrates→Plato→Aristotle

(6) **D.** The Peloponnesian War was fought when Athens tried to take over other city-states.

(7) **A.** Alexander the Great's death ended the Classical Period.

(8) **C.** The third and final period of Ancient Greece was the Hellenistic Period.

(9) **B.** There were twelve Olympians in Greek mythology.

(10) **B.** Homer wrote *The Odyssey* and *The Iliad.*

(11) **A.** The Greeks came up with trial by jury.

(12) **C.** The Greeks called themselves *hellens.*

(13) **B.** The ruler of the Greek gods was Zeus.

(14) **B.** An *acropolis* is an elevated area of land.

(15) **B.** The Ancient Greeks were polytheistic.

(16)   **True.** Alexander the Great was from Macedonia.

(17)   **True.** The Ancient Greeks used gods and goddesses to explain the way the world worked around them.

(18)   **False.** Athens did not win the Peloponnesian War; Sparta did.

(19)   **False.** Alexander the Great succeeded in spreading Greek culture during his conquests throughout Eurasia.

(20)   **False.** The Ancient Greeks did not conquer the Roman Empire; it was the other way around.

Ancient India: Quiz

(1) What theory says that humans came and traveled through Egypt and the Middle East, and spread across the world?
(A) Human Travel Theory
(B) Out-of-Africa Theory
(C) Egyptian Tunnel Theory
(D) Early Human Travel Theory

(2) What continent is India part of?
(A) Europe
(B) Asia
(C) Eastern Europe
(D) Middle East

(3) What mountains tower over the northeastern part of India?
(A) The Rocky Mountains
(B) The Misty Mountains
(C) The Himalayan Mountains
(D) The Alpian Mountains

(4) What was the *first* significant Indian empire?
(A) Mughal
(B) Guptan
(C) Harappan
(D) Buddhist

(5) What country is *not* included in the Indus Valley?
(A) India
(B) Pakistan

(C) Iran

(D) Turkey

(6) Which of the following empires did *not* conquer India?

(A) Mongolian

(B) Persian

(C) Greek

(D) Egyptian

(7) The Persians conquered India—who then conquered the Persians?

(A) Alexander the Great

(B) Babur

(C) Buddha

(D) Genghis Khan

(8) Who staged an Indian revolution and took Indian lands back from Greece?

(A) Buddha

(B) Genghis Khan

(C) Chandragupta II

(D) Chandragupta

(9) Chandragupta II started *what* empire in India?

(A) Mauryan

(B) Guptan

(C) Mugal

(D) Guptianian

(10) Who led the Mongols against India?

(A) Buddha

(B) Genghis Khan

(C) Chandragupta

(D) Alexander the Great

(11) What network of roads connected Asia and the Middle East?

(A) The Kingsroad
(B) The Egyptian Road
(C) The Silk Road
(D) The Iron Road

(12)   What does the word *Mughal* mean?
(A) It was the name of the Indian rebel-ruled empire
(B) It was the Indian word for *Mongol*
(C) It was what the Indians called themselves
(D) It was the main Indian export to China

(13)   What importance did sugar have to India?
(A) It was used during their religious services
(B) It served as the basis of *all* India's popular foods
(C) It was a main Indian export to China
(D) A lack of sugar eventually led to the fall of the Mauryan Empire

(14)   Which of the following was *not* one of India's central religions at one point?
(A) Judaism
(B) Hinduism
(C) Islam
(D) Buddhism

(15)   What do the Muslims call their god?
(A) Mughal
(B) God
(C) Allah
(D) Babur

(16)   Both Hindus and Buddhists believe in reincarnation.
(A) True
(B) False

(17)   India endured almost a thousand of years
     of foreign rule.
     (A) True
     (B) False

(18)   India was never ruled by its own people.
     (A) True
     (B) False

(19)   Gunpowder and guns were invented in
     England, and spread to Asia.
     (A) True
     (B) False

(20)   Sugar was used primarily in India, and
     spread to other places.
     (A) True
     (B) False

Ancient India: Quiz Answers

(1) **B.** The Out-of-Africa theory says that humans traveled through Egypt and the Middle East and spread throughout the world.

(2) **B.** India is part of the Asian continent.

(3) **C.** The Himalayan Mountains are in northeastern India.

(4) **C.** The Harappan Empire was the first significant Indian empire.

(5) **D.** Turkey is not included in the Indus Valley.

(6) **D.** The Egyptians did not conquer India.

(7) **A.** Alexander the Great conquered the Persians.

(8) **D.** Chandragupta staged an Indian revolution and took lands back from Greece.

(9) **C.** Chandragupta started the Guptan Empire in India.

(10) **B.** Genghis Khan led the Mongols against India.

(11) **C.** The Silk Road connected Asia and the Middle East.

(12) **B.** *Mughal* is the Indian word for Mongol.

(13) **C.** Sugar was a main Indian export to China.

(14) **A.** Judaism was not a central religion in India.

(15) **C.** Muslims call their god Allah.

(16) **True.** Both Hindus and Muslims believe in reincarnation.

(17)   **True.** India endured about a thousand years of foreign rule.

(18)   **False.** India was indeed ruled by its own people on occasion.

(19)   **False.** Gunpowder and guns were invented in Asia.

(20)   **True.** Sugar was perfected in India, and spread elsewhere.

Ancient China: Quiz

(1) What Asian country is bigger than China?
   (A) Korea
   (B) Russia
   (C) Mongolia
   (D) India

(2) Which of the following bodies of water does NOT border China?
   (A) Yellow Sea
   (B) East China Sea
   (C) South China Sea
   (D) Bay of Bengal

(3) What mountain range sits on the border between India and China?
   (A) The Alps
   (B) The Mountains of the Moon
   (C) The Himalayas
   (D) The Gobi Mountains

(4) Who were the Lungshan?
   (A) The warriors from Mongolia that repeatedly invaded China
   (B) The people who existed in Chinese lands before the Xia Dynasty
   (C) The group of scholars who invented gunpowder

(D) The builders who worked on the Great
Wall of China and the Forbidden City

(5) Which dynasty *first* created the Mandate of
Heaven, which decreed the gods gave them
the right to rule?
(A) Xia
(B) Qin
(C) Chou
(D) Shang

(6) Construction of the Great Wall of China
began during what dynasty?
(A) Xia
(B) Qin
(C) Chou
(D) Shang

(7) Why was the Great Wall of China built?
(A) To stop the Chinese people from
emigrating to Mongolia
(B) To stop the Chinese people from dying in
the Gobi Desert
(C) To create a walkway connecting the
Yellow Sea and central China
(D) To create a barricade, keeping the
Mongolian invaders out

(8) During what dynasty did the Silk Road
bloom?
(A) Han
(B) Ming
(C) Song
(D) Chou

(9) What major European empire desired China's abundance of silk and spices?
(A) Greek
(B) Egyptian
(C) Taklamakan
(D) Roman

(10) What was the Age of Division?
(A) A period during which many people were torn between supporting the Xia or the Ming Dynasty
(B) A period during which China almost split into two different countries, Gobi and Taklamakan
(C) A period during which the Chinese kingdoms fought each other for power
(D) A period during which the Chinese and Mongolian kingdoms battled for control of the Korean Peninsula

(11) When the Tang Dynasty rose to power, China entered the _____.
(A) Age of Division
(B) Era of Good Feeling
(C) Age of Heroes
(D) Golden Age

(12) What two inventions became popular as China moved into the Golden Age?
(A) Gunpowder and tea
(B) Scrolls and coffee
(C) Sugar and silk
(D) Bows and arrows

(13)	What was the Forbidden City initially used for?
  (A) A secret training center for Chinese soldiers
  (B) A hideout for Chinese royalty during times of war
  (C) The place from where Chinese royalty ruled
  (D) The place where China centered all of their riches and wealth, to stop the Mongolians from stealing it; hence, the "Forbidden" City

(14)	During what dynasty did the Forbidden City come about?
  (A) Xia
  (B) Tang
  (C) Chou
  (D) Ming

(15)	What people to the north continually invaded Chinese lands?
  (A) The Russians
  (B) The Mongolians
  (C) The Gobis
  (D) The Koreans

(16)	The Great Wall of China was completed during the Qin Dynasty.
  (A) True
  (B) False

(17)   The Himalayas were easily passable to Chinese travelers.
(A) True
(B) False

(18)   The Chinese kingdoms were often at odds with each other, especially during the Age of Division.
(A) True
(B) False

(19)   The Silk Road is called so, because China only wished to trade silk with Rome.
(A) True
(B) False

(20)   The Xia Dynasty was China's first dynasty.
(A) True
(B) False

Ancient China: Quiz Answers

(1) **B.** Russia is bigger than China.

(2) **D.** The Bay of Bengal does not border China.

(3) **C.** The Himalayas sit on the border between India and China.

(4) **B.** The Lungshan were the people who existed on Chinese lands before the Xia Dynasty.

(5) **D.** The Shang Dynasty *first* created the Mandate to Heaven, and the Chou used it after them.

(6) **B.** Construction of the Great Wall of China began during the Qin Dynasty.

(7) **D.** The Great Wall was built to keep Mongolian invaders out.

(8) **A.** The Silk Road bloomed during the Han Dynasty.

(9) **D.** The Roman Empire desired China's abundance of silk and spices.

(10)   **C.** The Age of Division was a period during which the Chinese kingdoms fought each other for power.

(11)   **D.** When the Tang Dynasty rose to power, China entered the Golden Age.

(12)   **A.** As China moved into the Golden Age, gunpowder and tea became popular.

(13)   **C.** The Forbidden City was initially the city from where Chinese royalty ruled.

(14)   **D.** The Forbidden City came about during the Ming Dynasty.

(15)   **B.** The Mongolians continually invaded Chinese lands.

(16)   **False.** The Great Wall was not built during the Qin Dynasty; it took 1700 years to build.

(17)   **False.** The Himalayas were not easy to pass for Chinese travelers.

(18)   **True.** The Chinese kingdoms were often at odds with each other, especially during the Age of Division.

(19)   **False.** The Silk Road was not given that name because China only wanted to trade silk with Rome.

(20)   **True.** The Xia Dynasty was China's first dynasty.

Ancient Rome: Quiz

(1) The city of Rome exists in what modern-day country?
(A) England
(B) Spain
(C) Greece
(D) Italy

(2) Which of the following was one of the names of Rome's mythical founders?
(A) Lupin
(B) Nero
(C) Caesar
(D) Romulus

(3) What happened to King Tarquin the Proud?
(A) He was overthrown by the Roman people.
(B) He was put into power by the Roman people, following a rebellion.
(C) He was assassinated by Julius Caesar.
(D) He was killed in the Coliseum by a gladiator.

(4) What group ruled the Roman Republic?
(A) The Roman Congress
(B) The Roman Empire
(C) The Roman Senate
(D) The Roman Patricians

(5) Who was the leader of the Roman gods?
(A) Zeus
(B) Poseidon
(C) Ares
(D) Jupiter

(6) What was the Roman lower class called?
(A) Plebeians
(B) Patricians
(C) Consuls
(D) Hobos

(7) The Punic Wars were fought between Rome and _____.
(A) Gaul
(B) The Visigoths
(C) Julius Caesar
(D) Carthage

(8) What Carthaginian general led his soldiers and dozens of elephants through the dangerous Alps?
(A) Julius Caesar
(B) Tarquin the Proud
(C) Hannibal
(D) Romulus

(9) What was Julius Caesar's fate?
(A) He was sent into the Coliseum to face a lion.
(B) He was stabbed repeatedly by Roman senators.
(C) He died of old age after successfully turning Rome into an empire.

(D) He was murdered by his nephew Octavian, who wanted the throne.

(10)   According to historians, which Roman leader was the first true *emperor*?
(A) Julius Caesar
(B) Tarquin the Proud
(C) Romulus
(D) Augustus

(11)   What religion did Emperor Constantine adopt?
(A) Judaism
(B) Buddhism
(C) Christianity
(D) Islam

(12)   In what structure did the Roman gladiators battle?
(A) The Coliseum
(B) The Senate
(C) The Fighting Pit
(D) The Plebeian

(13)   To which tribe did Emperor Valens extend an allyship?
(A) The Visigoths
(B) The Gauls
(C) The French
(D) The Vikings

(14)   Why did this tribe eventually turn on the Romans?
(A) The Romans tried to slaughter them.

(B) The Romans could not pay them money.
(C) The Romans insulted them at a feast.
(D) The Romans were planning to annihilate their leader at a wedding.

(15)   Which was NOT one of the reasons that the Roman Empire fell?
(A) Corrupt politicians
(B) Failing economy
(C) Invading barbarians
(D) The discovery of the New World

(16)   Rome was an Empire, and then a Republic.
(A) True
(B) False

(17)   The Romans had twelve main gods, as did the Greeks.
(A) True
(B) False

(18)   The Carthaginians overcame the Romans during the Punic Wars.
(A) True
(B) False

(19)   Julius Caesar was viewed by all as a great leader.
(A) True
(B) False

(20)   The Visigoths sacked the city of Rome.
(A) True

(B) False

Ancient Rome: Quiz Answers

(1) **D.** The city of Rome exists in modern-day Italy.

(2) **D.** Romulus was one of Rome's mythical founders.

(3) **A.** Tarquin the Proud was overthrown by the Roman people.

(4) **C.** The Roman Senate ruled the Republic.

(5) **D.** Jupiter led the Roman gods.

(6) **A.** The Roman lower class was called plebeians.

(7) **D.** The Punic Wars were fought between Rome and Carthage.

(8) **C.** Hannibal led his soldiers across the Alps.

(9) **B.** Julius Caesar was stabbed repeatedly by Roman senators.

(10) **D.** Augustus was the first true emperor of Rome.

(11) **C.** Emperor Constantine adopted Christianity.

(12) **A.** Roman gladiators battled in the Coliseum.

(13) **A.** Emperor Valens extended an allyship to the Visigoths.

(14) **B.** The Visigoths turned on the Romans because the Romans could not pay them money.

(15) **D.** The discovery of the New World did not affect the fall of the Roman Empire.

(16)   **False.** Rome was a Republic, then an Empire.

(17)   **True.** The Romans had twelve main gods.

(18)   **False.** The Carthaginians did not overcome the Romans during the Punic Wars.

(19)   **False.** Julius Caesar was not viewed as a great leader by all.

(20)   **True.** The Visigoths sacked the city of Rome.